"Love is the only force capable of

transforming an enemy

into a friend."

Martin Luther King, Jr.

How To Get Along with Anyone*

*yes, even that person

by The AstroTwins
Ophira and Tali Edut

Visit The AstroTwins at
www.astrostyle.com and @astrotwins

Contents

Introduction

~~~

The secret of compatibility is in the distance between your zodiac signs.

You know that ONE person who can push your buttons like nobody else in the world? No matter how enlightened you are, every interaction with them reduces you to a frustrated mess. You scream in public. You cry in the bathroom. You rage to your friends.

Ugh! How did they get to you again?

— Introduction —

Then there are your kindred spirits, the people with whom you just instantly click. There's no need to explain yourself; it's like you've known each other for lifetimes. (Surprise: maybe you have. More on that in a sec.)

It would be great if we could just fill the world with soulmates and ship the "difficult people" off to some desert island. Unfortunately, they often happen to be our parents, children, bosses, coworkers, spouses...people with whom our lives are inextricably intertwined.

It's sink or swim. You've got to make it work. And that's where astrology can help.

If you're reading this, chances are, you've heard the generic astrology compatibility tips. "I'm a Cancer, she's a Scorpio. We're both water signs, so we're perfect for each other!" Or, "He's a Virgo and I'm an Aquarius—that's a terrible match, I've heard. I really like him, but we probably shouldn't date, right?"

Wrong.

Studying and practicing astrology for over 20 years, we've come to believe that everyone is in your life for a reason. And that reason is encoded in the angle between your signs. Astrology is based on angles (called "aspects" in astro-speak), each one creating a unique interpersonal dynamic.

"SOME ASPECTS DO MAKE FOR

A SMOOTHER RELATIONSHIP,

BUT WE'VE LEARNED:

EASY DOESN'T NECESSARILY

MEAN GOOD."

— Introduction —

Some aspects do make for a smoother relationship, but here's something else we've learned: Easy doesn't necessarily mean good. Certainly, you need kindred spirits to reflect your highest self back to you. But sometimes, you need a challenge in order to evolve. The person who pushes you out of your comfort zone, or mirrors your own inner struggles, can be a powerful teacher. Often, we attract "difficult people" unconsciously because our souls yearn to grow. We need to wake up, pay attention, learn something. So don't shoot the messenger—even if he is a Capricorn (or whatever sign you've put on your cosmic s--t list).

As twins, we've been lifelong students of interpersonal dynamics. It's the nature of being born this way (cue the Lady Gaga). Sure, we've had our spats. But we've also been negotiating differences since the crib, where we shared toys and even invented our own language. We cut our coexisting teeth on years of birthday parties, when friends gave us "shared presents"—as if we were each half a person. (Trust us: one memorable fight over a Snoopy Sno-Cone Machine in 1979 taught us the power of compromise.)

We wrote this guide to help you understand WHY. Why are these tear-your-hair-out, frustrating relationships in your life? We say it's because there's something for you to learn. The suffering and friction and conflict...well, it ceases to be as big of an issue when you understand that person's purpose in your life on a karmic or

"WHY ARE THESE TEAR-
YOUR- HAIR-OUT,
FRUSTRATING RELATIONSHIPS
IN YOUR LIFE? BECAUSE
THERE'S SOMETHING FOR
YOU BOTH TO LEARN."

— Introduction —

soul level. You stop trying to change them and you quit pretending to be someone you're not. You can say, "This is what I'm dealing with here. Do I accept it or not?" The power is back in your hands.

As astrologers, we're all about helping you make a conscious choice from an informed place. That's what we love about astrology. It gives you a map, but YOU are always the driver. So here are a few things we've learned on our own journeys, through trial and observation, through hurled objects and weepy reconciliations. May it bring you peace—yes, even with that person. ✳

When You're

THE SAME SIGN

— Same Sign —

ENERGY: SELF-ACCEPTANCE
* ASPECT NAME: CONJUNCT

As they say, how can you love somebody else unless you love yourself? You'll find out exactly how deep your self-love runs when you tangle with a signmate. It's like looking in the mirror: On a good day, you steal a few extra glances at the hottie smiling back. Yeah, baby! But when your hair is a wreck or an "adult acne" outbreak strikes, the last thing you want to see is your own reflection.

When a signmate mirrors your better traits, you find yourself high-fiving, feeling validated and laughing aloud with recognition. When they present the ugly truth about your own flaws—or demonstrate a raw, unevolved trait that's common to your sign—you just want to run and hide.

For example, as outspoken Sagittarians, we know that our sign has a rep for bluntness. We adore the refreshing honesty and outrageous humor of a fellow Sag...to a point. But put two of us in a tight relationship, and we're either wetting our pants in the street from laughing or we're in each other's faces preaching about how to live...until the conversation escalates into a heated fight.

— Same Sign —

Cringe-inducing confession: Years ago, Ophi slapped a fellow Sagittarius (and to this day, a dear friend—thank God we're a forgiving sign) across the face when he wouldn't stop a barrage of unsolicited business advice. The slap literally echoed down a New York City block. Yet, who was often guilty of sledge-hammering her own friends and family with know-it-all "coaching" on many an occasion? (Meek hand-raise from Ophi.)

Essential Skills For This Relationship

Embrace the spectrum.

With any zodiac sign, there are a spectrum of qualities from "good" to "bad." Give yourselves room to express the whole range. One day, that fellow Cancer will morph into a moody bee-yotch, instead of being a caring confidante who spoils you with home-cooked meals. The next day, roles reverse, and you're the cranky "cat lady" throwing hot grits at your honey because they didn't make the bed. It's just the way it goes.

Bring in a third party to balance it out.

Sometimes, too much of a good thing is just...too much. Signmates may find it helpful to have a third person (of another sign) mediate conflict and ease your dynamic. For instance, two airy Geminis who bring out each other's flaky sides can benefit from the grounding impact of an earthy Virgo friend. Or, two workaholic Capricorn

"SAME-SIGN COUPLES MIGHT FIND IT EASY TO DISAPPEAR INTO A BUBBLE-FOR-TWO, BUT THIS CAN EVENTUALLY BACKFIRE. AUTONOMY IS IMPORTANT TO KEEP THE FRICTION ALIVE."

business partners might appreciate having a playful Leo assistant who reminds them to go have fun.

And who can forget the double-Leo relationship between Ben Affleck and Jennifer Lopez known as "Bennifer"? The pop-culture world still has a collective hangover from their spray-tanned, blinged-out lifestyle of sappy romantic gestures, 6.1-carat Harry Winston pink diamond engagement rings and over-the-top gifts. (Never mind the romance-a-holic Leonine ode "Dear Ben" that she crooned while we cringed—or the flopped film Gigli that stained their careers.) Perhaps if Matt Damon had stepped in with some balanced Libra perspective, their fizzled fairytale could have ended differently.

Same-sign couples might find it easy to disappear into a bubble-for-two, but this can eventually backfire. Autonomy is important to keep the friction alive. Hanging with other people creates healthy separation between your identities. Otherwise, passion can cool to a brother-sister vibe.

Own your quirks.
If you haven't learned to love yourself, warts and all, this relationship can inspire some crucial self-acceptance. If you find yourself pissed off by every little thing a signmate does, check in: Is it because you do these things too and are in denial about

— Same Sign —

it? Is this person reminding you of some not-so-distant mistakes you've made that you're still beating yourself up for? Or are they expressing some traits you feel ashamed about in yourself?

Chances are, your irksome signmate is revealing an exaggerated version of your "flaws," and you feel exposed. Like that fellow Virgo who sends back every dish she orders at a restaurant and whips out the Purell sanitizer after shaking your hand. Or that other Taurus who name-drops and demands to know the vineyard and vintage of any wine before taking a sip. So maybe you only send back every tenth meal, or just quietly order the same Pinot Noir and swirl it to check its "legs." If someone could put your thoughts on loudspeaker, they'd totally hear you obsessing about germs when people hug you, or judging your friend for ordering a "house zinfandel" and not knowing what the word sommelier means. Yeah, it's neurotic, embarrassing and kind of weird. So what? Own it. ✳

LESSONS OF THIS RELATIONSHIP

• To see your best and worst qualities mirrored back
• Self-acceptance
• Working through sibling rivalry
• Getting past self-consciousness
• Owning your authentic quirks

When You're

ONE SIGN

APART

— One Sign Apart —

ENERGY: FRICTION, DIFFERENCE
* ASPECT: SEMISEXTILE

meet your matches

Aries: Taurus, Pisces

Taurus: Aries, Gemini

Gemini: Taurus, Cancer

Cancer: Gemini, Leo

Leo: Cancer, Virgo

Virgo: Leo, Libra

Libra: Virgo, Scorpio

Scorpio: Libra, Sagittarius

Sagittarius: Scorpio, Capricorn

Capricorn: Sagittarius, Aquarius

Aquarius: Capricorn, Pisces

Pisces: Aries, Aquarius

— One Sign Apart —

L ike next-door neighbors with a completely different style of decorating, gardening and living, the signs on either side of yours can stir up an instant love-hate vibe. Signs that are semisextile or inconjunct (as this angle is called) to each other have no astrological traits in common. For example, one of you is a fire sign, the other is earth element; one is yin and the other yang; one is a flexible "mutable" sign while the other is a stubborn "fixed" or "cardinal" quality.

Of course, all that friction can lead to explosive sexual chemistry, even an obsessive desire to figure each other out (heads-up: you never completely will). Some astrologers believe that each sign is an evolved version of the one before it. According to that theory, the sign after yours plays the role of a teacher—although your pride may never allow you to admit it until years later.

This combination can make for painful breakups, and a seething sexual tension that lingers for a lifetime. ("I can't quit ya!") Mostly, it's because you never figure each other out, no matter how many fights, self-help books and therapy sessions you endure. As Sagittarians, we've both been in infuriating romantic relationships with Scorpios and Capricorns that still feel a little unresolved years later. As hard as we tried, there was never any true closure—and with one-sign-apart relationships, that's something you learn to accept.

— One Sign Apart —

But what happens in the bedroom is a far cry from the boardroom. In business relationships, the one-sign-apart dynamic can be fantastic. This is where differences can actually be an asset. Say you're a Taurus business type who loves money and hates marketing. Team up with an Aries PR maven and a Gemini social media whiz. While you decorate your corner office and write corporate bylaws, they'll score you 50,000 Twitter followers and an interview on the five o' clock news.

Still, this cosmic combo comes with a warning label: you must each carve out your own turf and be crystal-clear about roles. We learned this the hard way during a joint business venture with a Scorpio years ago. At the outset, she admired our grand Sagittarian vision, and we loved her hawklike attention to the financial bottom line. Until, that is, she wanted us to work in an office 9-to-5 (death to the Sag free spirit!) and analyze weekly profit-and-loss spreadsheets printed in (no kidding) five-point Times New Roman type.

With typical Sagittarian impulsiveness, Ophi moved to a remote, chilly northern Minnesota town for six months as part of this business deal. She only discovered their different daily work styles after settling into a damp apartment on the same street as a taxidermy shop and a run-down casino. It was an intense time, but also a period of incredible self-discovery. In hindsight, we're grateful for the experience, though it certainly wasn't easy.

— One Sign Apart —

Essential Skills For This Relationship

Get over yourself.

So you think your way is the right way, the only way, the best way to do things? Think again. Mastering a semisextile relationship means admitting that someone else's "standard operating procedure" is equally valid to yours—even when it's wildly different. This can be humbling to the ego, and you'll need to swallow your pride on a regular basis. Adopt a firm "I'm okay, you're okay" or "live and let live" stance. There will be times when you'll need to agree to disagree, and even take cooling-off periods.

Heap on the praise.

When you feel jealous or threatened by your differences, don't compete. Give a compliment instead. Yeah, this is the last thing you'll want to do when you're upset. Make an effort to praise each other often during the good times—for reinforcement's sake. When you're in the midst of a teary-eyed brawl, at least there's a chance you'll remember the love.

This technique also helps you appreciate your differences (since there are many), rather than viewing them as a threat. Your semisextile partner is really good in areas where you're weak—and vice-versa. So make sure to go the extra mile and acknowledge each other for that. The positive reinforcement will be balm to your

"WHEN YOU FEEL JEALOUS

OR THREATENED BY

YOUR DIFFERENCES,

DON'T COMPETE. GIVE A

COMPLIMENT INSTEAD."

souls. And it will be a brilliant exercise in setting your ego aside, which will help your souls grow.

Be the "top" AND the "bottom."
Because your personalities are so distinct, you'll need to take turns being the "alpha" in the relationship. One leads, the other supports—and vice-versa. Otherwise, this can quickly devolve into a rivalry, with two triggered egos battling for the upper hand.

Forget about "healthy competition."
In a sextile relationship, there really is none. Sure, you can inspire each other to be better people, but jealousy can easily flare. Look within and ask: Why is this person my nemesis? Maybe I feel like I'm lacking something because I don't have what they have. Then, remember that you, too, have amazing talents that your semisextile person doesn't. What if you combine your superpowers instead of trying to zap each other's?

Groundrules may need to be established and verbalized.
In a semisextile dynamic, it's probably important to have a no-interrupting policy, so each person can fully voice their ideas before the other one shoots it down. "You're not listening to me" or "You don't understand me" can be common refrains. Make a dedicated effort to give each other equal airtime, and really consider the perspectives shared.

— One Sign Apart —

Respect each other's turf, too.

If one of you is especially awesome at picking restaurants, for example, then the other should stay off Yelp and let the foodie make the damn reservations. Set your ego aside and let each other shine. Following a 50/50 rule doesn't always work in semisextile pairings. (Otherwise, you'll go to crappy restaurants half the time!) What's most important here is that you both define your assets and step out of each other's way.

Spending time together or collaborating on a project can be the glue that keeps semisextile relationships humming. Since you may lack enough common personality traits, you'll need to bond through shared experiences instead. Play to your winning individual strengths, and together, you'll take over the world!

Dare to be yourself.

Validation doesn't come easily in a one-sign-apart relationship. You're usually too busy trying to figure each other out, or to find some common ground. So guess what? You've got to validate yourself. Be bold about asserting your opinions, needs and beliefs. In this relationship, nobody is a mind-reader, so you've got to spell it out in black-and-white. This will take courage, as you may be afraid of baring your soul to an unappreciative audience. Learning courage is one of this relationship's biggest benefits, though—so step up to the plate and voice your truth! ✸

"MASTERING THIS RELATIONSHIP MEANS ADMITTING THAT SOMEONE ELSE'S 'STANDARD OPERATING PROCEDURE' IS EQUALLY VALID TO YOURS—EVEN WHEN IT'S WILDLY DIFFERENT."

— One Sign Apart —

LESSONS OF THIS RELATIONSHIP

- To see how the other side lives
- To team up with a mate who has qualities you don't (and vice versa)
- Deep healing and transformation, at times through painful growth
- To learn from each other's differences
- To force you out of your fear-based comfort zone or emotional paralysis
- Growth through challenge or contrast
- How to assert yourself with someone who doesn't instantly "get" you
- Making peace with "the enemy"

When You're

TWO

SIGNS

APART

— Two Signs Apart —

ENERGY: FRIENDSHIP, COMMUNICATION

* ASPECT: SEXTILE

meet your matches

Aries: Gemini, Aquarius

Taurus: Cancer, Pisces

Gemini: Aries, Leo

Cancer: Taurus, Virgo

Leo: Gemini, Libra

Virgo: Cancer, Scorpio

Libra: Leo, Sagittarius

Scorpio: Virgo, Capricorn

Sagittarius: Libra, Aquarius

Capricorn: Scorpio, Pisces

Aquarius: Aries, Sagittarius

Pisces: Taurus, Capricorn

— *Two Signs Apart* —

It's easy and breezy to be around people who live two zodiac signs away. Your signs are always of a compatible "element" (for example, one of you is a Water sign and the other is an Earth sign). Thus, you'll have similar values and attitudes about everything: food, music, politics, family, which movies to rent. The lack of self-consciousness you feel around each other makes it easy to take new risks. You feel comfortable lounging around bra-less reading the Sunday paper, or peeing with the door open.

Friendship and communication are the hallmarks of this aspect. You're the duo that could go on Survivor or The Amazing Race and smoke the competition because you're so in sync. You play well together, so you make fabulous party co-hosts if your circles overlap. Business ventures between these signs are favorable, too, since you bring out each other's creativity and productivity.

Being best friends is easy. Keeping the spark alive? A little challenging. Sextile couples need to structure "date nights" or set up scenarios that get you out of buddy mode and well, put the "sex" back in "sextile." Friends and coworkers need to consciously introduce new topics and activities to avoid falling into a glazed-eye rut.

— Two Signs Apart —

Essential Skills For This Relationship

Add spice liberally.

Here's a cautionary tale of two-signs-apart couple Jennifer Aniston (Aquarius) and Brad Pitt (Sagittarius). In their wedding vows, he promised to "split the difference on the thermostat" and she swore to always make his favorite banana milkshake. Cute. But the human soul craves a higher calling from our relationships than effortlessness. (To wit: even the best milkshake was no match for Pitt's attraction to an intriguing "citizen of the world" and her adopted global brood. #RIPBrangelina)

This astrological angle is one of friendships and siblings. No wonder Brad and Jen's black-and-white wedding album and red carpet photos were so captivating: They look like brother and sister! After the excitement of discovering you have everything in common, sextile life together can get kind of flat and predictable. The two-signs-apart couple can avoid the "Braniston" trap by proactively introducing life-expanding ideas into the relationship. Sharing new restaurants, movies, vacations and intellectually stimulating experiences can keep things fresh.

Friends, siblings and coworkers who are two signs apart can devolve into "sibling rivalry" at times, working each other's nerves in that too-close-for-comfort way. The issue: You feel so at ease around each other that you may take each other for granted. For years, we made the egregious error of not attending a Libra writer friend's book signings, figuring she wouldn't miss us. A decade later, we found that we'd deeply hurt her feelings. Lesson learned: better to put forth the effort than have a messy cleanup later.

Use body language, not buddy language.

Dude. Bruh. Man. Homie. The first syllable of each other's names. Whatever your impersonal nicknames are, the football locker room talk will make this relationship feel like more like The Hangover than a cherished connection. Yeah, it's fun to punch each other's arms and tease like teenage siblings. But remember, sibling relationships can also be cruel. Make an effort to compliment each other, even if it feels silly, awkward and formal. If you're a couple, skip the cutesie nicknames and baby talk—or at least cut back on it.

Have a common enemy or gripe.

Okay, we don't really recommend this as a long-term strategy, because y'know, it's kind of a time-waster to bond over bitching. But the power of this relationship is in your synergistic worldviews and easy dialogue. Just when you've run out of things to talk about and are about to start bickering or neglecting each other—bam. Along comes that person whose outrageous self-centeredness offends

"AFTER THE EXCITEMENT OF DISCOVERING YOU HAVE EVERYTHING IN COMMON, SEXTILE LIFE TOGETHER CAN GET KIND OF FLAT AND PREDICTABLE."

you both for the same reasons. Who can dissect the episode blow by blow better than your two-signs-away buddy? Nobody.

A less toxic version of this is sharing a laugh over a quirky observation. We have this dynamic with our Libra sister Leora, who is two signs away from us. Although we fight all the usual sibling turf wars, we get hysterical imitating our parents' quirky Eastern European friends (accents and all) or making up ridiculously snarky song lyrics about wacky situations we encounter. These inside jokes are our go-to tension relievers when we've been fighting over the remote control or who ate the last carton of Chinese food leftovers. ✳

— Two Signs Apart —

LESSONS OF THIS RELATIONSHIP

- How to be "best friends with benefits"
- The possibility of great communication
- How to speak up, listen, and be heard
- How to keep the spark going when it stops automatically lighting itself
- Romance forming naturally out of friendship
- A no-pressure gig with someone who doesn't demand more than you can give

When You're

THREE

SIGNS

APART

— Three Signs Apart —

ENERGY: CHALLENGE, COMPETITION, DYNAMIC BALANCE

* ASPECT: SQUARE

meet your matches

Aries: Cancer, Capricorn

Taurus: Leo, Aquarius

Gemini: Virgo, Pisces

Cancer: Aries, Libra

Leo: Taurus, Scorpio

Virgo: Gemini, Sagittarius

Libra: Cancer, Capricorn

Scorpio: Leo, Aquarius

Sagittarius: Virgo, Pisces

Capricorn: Aries, Libra

Aquarius: Taurus, Scorpio

Pisces: Gemini, Sagittarius

— Three Signs Apart —

Power! Passion! Intrigue! Your signs form a harsh, 90-degree angle to each other called a square, creating a push-pull dynamic. There can be power struggles and clashing agendas—along with an undeniable chemistry. Don't expect to kick back and put your feet up in a square relationship. Three signs apart duos keep you on your toes, in constant negotiation and dialogue. The tension makes you active and keyed up. Of course, that could be exactly what you want (or a wild turn-on!). The opportunity of the "square" aspect is to teach you how to compromise with an equally strong-willed partner. When you strike that delicate balance, you can make an indomitable "power couple"—a true force to be reckoned with. A few notable examples: Bill and Hillary Clinton. Jennifer Lopez and P. Diddy. Arnold Schwarzenegger and Maria Shriver. Yeah, they all ended up with scandalous People magazine cover stories. But when they combined their willpower and resources, they were untouchable, head-turning duos who nobody wanted to mess with.

Got mommy and daddy issues? The square relationship helps you work through baggage from a difficult parent, sometimes by reactivating old, painful wounds. That's because your signs rule the fourth house (the mother sector) and the tenth house (the father zone) of each other's charts. It's even possible that you were each other's parent or child in a past life, and have reunited for another karmic go-round.

— Three Signs Apart —

You may very well enter each other's lives to heal those parent-child issues. As Sagittarians, we've had profound relationships with Virgos and Pisces. These relationships both healed and triggered some abandonment fears we didn't even know we had. The breakups were rough, and definitely took a few rounds of back-and-forth to really cut the cord.

The saving grace of your three signs apart combo? Your signs share the same astrological "quality." You're both either a flexible mutable sign, a stubborn fixed sign, or a leadership-driven cardinal sign. For this reason, you'll share some common values and approaches to life. The trick is to balance the proportions, so that you don't step on each other's toes.

Essential Skills For This Relationship

Take turns leading and following.
You know the saying about too many cooks being in the kitchen? One of you is gonna have to ditch those "chef's whites" to avoid stirring the pot or ruining dinner. Otherwise, you can end up jockeying for control instead of playing to your strengths.

Clear communication and expectations, outlined to the letter, also help. So you need two days apart minimum each week? You want to keep your own homes instead of moving in together? Whatever

"WHETHER IN LOVE, WORK, OR FRIENDSHIP, THE CAPACITY FOR NEEDINESS IS VAST IN THIS COMBINATION, SO YOU MUST BE CONSCIOUS NOT TO DUMP YOUR DRAMA ON EACH OTHER."

works. It's best to spell out these needs clearly upfront—and to willingly meet each other halfway.

That said, there may come a time when you have to give something up for the greater good of the relationship. In a square, unlike in other combinations, it needs to be painstakingly 50/50, split down the middle equally. Otherwise, resentment can set in, eroding the relationship to the point of destruction. To wit: Both Bill and Hillary Clinton ran for United States President, campaigning tirelessly for one another when they did.

Deal with your "primal wounds."
So, your mother was cold and aloof. Your parents divorced when you were ten. Dad hit the road and remarried, leaving you feeling unwanted. Mm-hmmm. You can either work through that with a therapist, or you can reenact the dynamic with each other. (We recommend the former.)

Whether in love, work, or friendship, the capacity for neediness is vast in this combination, so you must be conscious not to dump your drama on each other. Notice when you're acting like a bratty kid or lecturing like a nagging parent. If you're the parental one, practice the art of loving detachment and set clear boundaries. If you're being the whiny baby, step up your level of personal responsibility. Otherwise, the relationship can become a burden.

— Three Signs Apart —

A little refresher course on codependence might be helpful, too.

Many three signs apart couples discover their differences when they become parents together. Don't wait for this to happen. Discuss your vision for child-rearing beforehand, as compromise will surely be necessary. And by all means, deal with your own unresolved parent issues as much as possible before you procreate.

Strive for a common goal.

The competitive fires can't be quelled, so might as well use them to your advantage. Funnel that restless, go-getter energy into a shared challenge. Start a business. Sign up for a marathon or a Mt. Everest climb. Run for office and hit the campaign trail together. Just make sure you have clearly defined roles and responsibilities. That way, you can both shine...without outshining each other.

Having no shared agenda can seriously weaken the bond in three signs apart pairings. Ophi and her college boyfriend, a Virgo, shared an interest in spirituality, and spent hours at the bookstore (fave stomping grounds for lifelong learners Virgo and Sag). It was a profound two-year relationship that ran really deep, despite the fact that they only saw each other on the weekend and lived two hours apart. Things were rosy while they were doing "space clearings" with sage wands or performing full moon rituals. But when Mr. Virgo decided to be initiated into a West African religious tradition, their paths diverged. The breakup was painful, and in hindsight, felt like losing a family member. With a square relationship, you sometimes "don't know what you've got 'til it's gone." But the good part? You usually leave the relationship wiser and self-aware. ✴

LESSONS OF THIS RELATIONSHIP

- How to be "best friends with benefits"
- Compromise
- Conflict resolution
- Balancing your dynamic, sometimes clashing, personalities
- Where you can be stubborn and unyielding
- Healing old wounds/baggage related to your parents

When You're

FOUR
SIGNS
APART

— Four Signs Apart —

ENERGY: HARMONY, EASE

* ASPECT: TRINE

meet your matches

FIRE
Aries: Leo, Sagittarius
Leo: Aries, Sagittarius
Sagittarius: Aries, Leo

AIR
Gemini: Libra, Aquarius
Libra: Gemini, Aquarius
Aquarius: Gemini, Libra

EARTH
Taurus: Virgo, Capricorn
Virgo: Taurus, Capricorn
Capricorn: Taurus, Virgo

WATER
Cancer: Scorpio, Pisces
Scorpio: Cancer, Pisces
Pisces: Cancer, Scorpio

— Four Signs Apart —

Couldn't getting along just be easy for once? Yes! You've done the bitter breakups, crash-and-burn friendships, and intense showdowns with those "difficult people." Now, you just want a break. Chances are, you'll find it with the person who lives four signs away. The trine sign shares the same element as you: you're both either fire, earth, air or water signs, positioned at a harmonious 120-degree angle away from each other on the horoscope wheel. This can create an unspoken kinship and harmony. At last, you don't have to constantly explain yourself or put on airs! It feels like coming home after a long journey—safe, comfortable and familiar.

But again, we must slap on the warning label: Easy doesn't necessarily mean better. Just because you can drop the niceties and let loose around each other—burping, farting, yanking out wedgies and skipping showers—doesn't mean you should. Because seriously, would you want to spend all your time around the person who picks their nose and flicks it behind the couch, or spends all day in a sweaty nightgown? No? Well, check the mirror, honey: that person could now be you.

Sharing an astrological element (fire, earth, air or water), as trines do, can also be "too much of a good thing." Our parents are both loud, temperamental fire signs who have been married 40 years. (Visiting their house might be easier with tranquilizers.)

— Four Signs Apart —

Our Sagittarius dad interrupts our Leo mom mid-sentence, but she keeps talking anyway, until the walls are echoing with words neither of them even hears. Being Sagittarians ourselves, we jump into the fray, which only adds to the noise levels. No wonder our poor Libra sister (the lone air sign in the house) blasted her radio as a kid—she needed a blaring bass hook to drown out our fire-sign madness.

Essential Skills For This Relationship

Make an effort (even if you don't have to).
The trouble with things that come easily is, we tend to take them for granted. Have you ever run around like a madman trying to please a difficult, demanding person—someone you don't even like that much? It's funny how we spend time appeasing bullies, sucking up to a--hole bosses, or bailing out that troubled relative yet again. And who gets shuffled to the bottom of the list? That devoted friend who's always so understanding, loyal and unconditionally loving. Often, this neglected soul is four signs away from yours—a tried-and-true trine.

In trine romantic relationships, you'll need to preserve some mystery to keep the spark alive. Otherwise, quicker than you can say "Easy Spirit," your wardrobe goes from low-rise jeans and thongs to worn-out Hanes Her Way granny panties and drawstring pants. Anyone remember when Sagittarius Britney Spears was dating Aries dancer Kevin Federline? It was 24/7 trucker caps, dirty white undershirts and bare feet in public bathrooms. And there was nary a potato chip or a Big Mac sold on America's highway exits that those two wouldn't devour.

The trine relationship offers the opportunity to reward the folks who treat us best...just because. Say thank you and express gratitude, even if you don't have to. Buy the cards and flowers. For years, our father, a Sagittarius landscaper, only brought our Leo mom the red roses she loved when he clipped them out of a customer's garden. (Cough up the cash, pops!) Now, our Libra sister forces him to give her funds for the florist, and she picks out the Mother's Days and birthday blooms.

Bust up the cosmic mafia.

Cliques can easily form when you're four signs apart, because it's just so damn easy and fun to be around each other. Trouble is, other people can feel excluded from all your inside jokes and conversations, or underrepresented in your planetary parliament. When it's time to vote on vacation spots or to make a business decision, those poor non-triners are always outnumbered. If you're surrounded by signs of your element and everything feels super insider-y, push yourself to be more tolerant of those who don't share your tastes, worldview, humor and values.

"CLIQUES CAN EASILY FORM

WHEN YOU'RE FOUR SIGNS

APART, BECAUSE IT'S JUST SO

DAMN EASY AND FUN TO BE

AROUND EACH OTHER."

— Four Signs Apart —

In a trine love relationship, it's so easy to be together, you don't really take a break. Then one day, you realize that the whole "absence makes the heart grow fonder" thing has its merits. Ophi's first live-in boyfriend was in Aries who had a nightly habit of watching either Lord of the Rings or Gladiator to "wind down." Two years later, Ophi could practically speak in Elvish, knew her way through Middle Earth by heart, and would occasionally yell "Maximuuuuus!" while raising an invisible spear in victory. A little too much couple time, ya think?

Small wonder that both Ophi and her ex were a good 20 pounds heavier by the time they broke up. A little autonomy goes a long way to keep the connection alive, whether you're friends, lovers or family members.

Introduce another kind of energy.
Too much of a good thing can just be...too much. If your pond is stocked with too many water signs (Cancer, Scorpio, Pisces), bring in a couple of adventurous fire signs (Aries, Leo, Sagittarius) to spice up the action. A predominance of air signs (Gemini, Libra, Aquarius) can become cool, scattered and emotionally detached. They can benefit from a splash or water or a bit of grounding earth sign (Taurus, Virgo, Capricorn) energy.

— Four Signs Apart —

There are four elements in the zodiac for a reason, and it's because we need this dynamic balance to create a healthy whole. Although we may gravitate to people of our element because we feel at home, too much of that creates cabin fever. Just as traveling to a foreign country carves a new dimension into our life experience, hanging with signs outside your element makes you more worldly and tolerant—a citizen of the universe. ✳

LESSONS OF THIS RELATIONSHIP

- How to be "best friends with benefits"
- To feel at home with yourself and a mate
- How let down your guard and be yourself
- To be understood without explaining yourself
- To rest and relax together
- To have a best friend and partner in one

······································

When You're

FIVE

SIGNS

APART

······································

— Five Signs Apart —

ENERGY: ADJUSTMENT, KARMIC LESSONS, COMPROMISE

* ASPECT: QUINCUNX

meet your matches

Aries: Virgo, Scorpio

Taurus: Libra, Sagittarius

Gemini: Scorpio, Capricorn

Cancer: Sagittarius, Aquarius

Leo: Capricorn, Pisces

Virgo: Aries, Aquarius

Libra: Taurus, Pisces

Scorpio: Aries, Gemini

Sagittarius: Taurus, Cancer

Capricorn: Gemini, Leo

Aquarius: Cancer, Virgo

Pisces: Leo, Libra

— Five Signs Apart —

This is a fascinating, complex combination that defies explanation—the original odd couple. From one moment to the next, you'll either feel like you're with a kindred spirit or a complete stranger, no matter how many years you've known each other. Your bond is intense, unspoken, and baffling even to you. It's as though you've always known each other, but you can't really figure out how. We believe this is the ultimate past-life reunion, when two people come together to sort out unfinished business.

Why is the quincunx combo so surreal? The person five signs away from your sign has nothing in common with you astrologically. For example, you're a masculine air sign, while they're a feminine water or earth sign. This is similar to the semisextile, or one sign apart, relationship in some ways. But the increased distance between your signs contributes even more to the chasm that can grow between you if you don't play this relationship right.

So, how can two wildly different souls come together? You'll need to adapt to your differences, which could take a great deal of adjustment, even discarding a former lifestyle (like moving to the country when you're a "city girl") or going without some of your usual creature comforts (you want a penthouse corner office; your business partner prefers to work from home in pajamas).

"WHY IS THE QUINCUNX COMBO SO SURREAL? THE PERSON FIVE SIGNS AWAY FROM YOUR SIGN HAS NOTHING IN COMMON WITH YOU ASTROLOGICALLY."

— Five Signs Apart —

This combo can also expose the raw, uncomfortable truth about power dynamics. Although we all like to sing kumbaya and pretend we want everything 50/50, in truth, unequal dynamics are part of every relationship. Sometimes, differences can be sexy or exciting, especially if you take on complementary roles.

Have you done your "spiritual work" yet? If you meet each other before conducting enough personal growth, this can be a highly combustible combo—and not in a good way. Timing is everything in a quincunx duo. Rivalries can spawn when five-signs-apart people meet early in their lives (as childhood sweethearts, family members or friends, for example). Young quincunx pairs may lack the necessary tools and maturity to handle their different communication and conflict management styles. The term "frenemy" was popularized when Aquarius heiress Paris (triple rhyme!) Hilton broke up with BFFs Nicole Richie (Virgo) and Lindsay Lohan (Cancer)—the two signs that are five spots away on the zodiac wheel. Coincidence? We think not. #QuincunxLife

But if you know thyself, this relationship could have a happy ending. The older and wiser you are, the easier quincunx relationships become. The quincunx person may be in and out of your life for years, as you come together for a karmic lesson or a specific purpose, then go your separate ways for a while. There may be teary-eyed reconciliations once you've both grown wiser from experience. Or, you could meet after you've both been through some heart-wrenching experience that forced you to grow and learn personal responsibility. In this case, you may simply appreciate your differences, rather than seeing them as a threat to your ego or worldview.

Essential skills for this relationship

Approach it like you're dealing with an alien ('cuz you kind of are). Imagine you met an extraterrestrial. You'd have zero expectations that he would speak your language, share your political beliefs, shop at your favorite boutiques or enjoy "long walks on the beach and comedy clubs," too.

Your quincunx buddy might as well have been dropped from the nearest UFO. If you can choose to find this "alien attraction" endearing rather than annoying—which will take a lot of practice— you can form a lifelong bond. You might even learn a thing or two from each other. Ophi, a shabby-chic and thrift store-loving Sagittarius, is married to a Taurus who (no kidding) owns a $300 Jil Sander bathing suit. He used to drive a Rolls Royce; she painted her high school jalopy in 1960s-inspired art and named it The Psychedelic Chariot. Had they met while in high school or their 20s, they definitely wouldn't have meshed. But because they came together after his divorce and her last eye-opening breakup, they were "ready" for each other. Remember again: Timing is everything in a quincunx match!

Know and love thyself.

There is no wiggle room for the unevolved here. These relationships seem to work best after both people have gone through a profound experience—divorce, death of a loved one, a bad but life-altering breakup, recovery from addiction—some kind of wakeup call that brought on extreme self-awareness. Owning your baggage and knowing your emotional triggers is a must. Otherwise, you'll spend the entire time trying to change each other, which only leaves you both feeling frustrated and invalidated.

Accept your status as "the odd couple."

Remember when Virgo Michael Jackson married Aquarius Lisa Marie Presley? If not, head to YouTube and watch their super-awkward "You Are Not Alone" video. Just see if you can sit through it without growing deeply uncomfortable. We can't.

In truth, people are going to judge you no matter what. But in quincunx pairings, it can get especially harsh, so you'll need a thick skin. We know at least two Gemini-Capricorn couples where the Gemini woman is the breadwinner, while the Cappy works part-time and plays stay-at-home dad (a rare move for the sign of the father and provider). We've heard people gossip about them, wondering

"THERE IS NO WIGGLE ROOM FOR THE UNEVOLVED HERE. THESE RELATIONSHIPS SEEM TO WORK BEST AFTER BOTH PEOPLE HAVE GONE THROUGH A PROFOUND EXPERIENCE."

— Five Signs Apart —

if he's a "kept man" who's only after her money. Alternately, the Geminis have been whispered about as man-eating cougars with boy toys. No, everyone: It's a quincunx thing—and you probably wouldn't understand.

Not only is this an unfair double standard, it's also the nature of a quincunx bond. To the outside world, the connection looks strange and inexplicable. But often, it totally works for the two of you—and that's what matters. If you're happy, who cares what people think?

Discover your common purpose.

Five signs apart duos are always brought together for a grander cosmic reason. You have something to learn from each other, or a special mission on earth that requires your unique differences. In many cases, you're meant to be parents together, and your children's souls have selected the two of you especially to shepherd them into the world. Barack Obama (a Leo) and Michelle Obama (a Capricorn) are a great example of a winning quincunx combo. He's the warm-hearted softie while she may be the quiet "iron fist in the velvet glove," but they clearly co-parented (and ran the country together) pretty well.

That's the advantage of being five signs apart: You're so different, that you don't really step on each other's turf. When two powerful people of this distance come together to raise kids, start a business, create art or coexist as relatives, you can bring your differing skillsets to create something amazing. But pack your magic decoder ring and plenty of patience...just in case. ✷

LESSONS OF THIS RELATIONSHIP

- Karmic repair and lessons
- Healing a "past life contract" with each other
- Exploring and expanding your sexuality
- Diving into deeper intimacy
- Developing your selfless side
- Learning to serve or give
- How to adjust to someone vastly different
- Knowing what it feels like to meet a soulmate

······························

When You're

SIX
SIGNS
APART

······························

— Six Signs Apart —

ENERGY: PERSPECTIVE, CONTRAST, BALANCE

* ASPECT: OPPOSITE

~

meet your matches

Aries: Libra

Taurus: Scorpio

Gemini: Sagittarius

Cancer: Capricorn

Leo: Aquarius

Virgo: Pisces

Libra: Aries

Scorpio: Taurus

Sagittarius: Gemini

Capricorn: Cancer

Aquarius: Leo

Pisces: Virgo

— Six Signs Apart —

Your opposite sign lives directly across the zodiac wheel from you. However, you've got more in common than the name suggests. This sign can be highly compatible, even a soul twin. You each have a distinct role, but you're a tag team, too. As the saying goes: Opposites attract!

With an opposite sign, you're challenged to grow as a person and take responsibility for your part of the relationship. It's like taking a big step back to get a clear perspective of your life. We tend to view things from close up, missing the whole picture by hyper-focusing on a detail or two. With an opposite sign, your life appears in full relief, like a finished painting. Suddenly, it all makes sense. This panomarmic view can be a little uncomfortable to take in, but it's definitely enlightening.

Essential Skills For This Relationship

Attract. Repel. Rinse and repeat.
Like two magnets, you can either attract or repel each other, depending on which side of yourself you show. There will be days when you feel like kindred spirits and soul twins, a perfect tag team. You like yoga and juicing? Omigod, I do, too! Or, Wait, I had no idea anyone else on earth read that obscure postmodern literary magazine besides me! The next minute, you realize that

while you may like the same foods, hobbies, books, movies and activities, you approach them in completely polar ways. For example, you might both love a vegetarian banquet, but one of you gorges it down in greedy gulps, while the other slowly nibbles at a tofu cutlet, then wraps up the rest for leftovers.

Our Taurus friend Kimberly (name changed to protect the not-so-innocent) described her first attempted makeout session with Josh, a Scorpio. Both signs can be lusty, but Taurus is the sign of sensuality, while Scorpio rules raw, down-and-dirty passion. Kim likes slow, sensual kisses. Actually, a whole warmup to the first kiss would be even better: some light touching, a candlelit massage, dinner followed by a flower delivery, even a demure game of footsie. Rushing is a total turnoff to Kim, but once she's in, she's in. She jokes that it take 15 hours to get her into bed, then 15 hours to get her out. (For Scorpio sexaholic Josh, it took about 15 minutes in both directions.)

So imagine Kim's shock after her first coffee date, when Josh dove at her mouth with his tongue like a guided missile. Later, he texted her a nearly-naked picture of himself doing a yoga pose (um, why?) and sent a stream of dirty-talking emails that would be hot to a Scorpio, but left her Taurus loins cold. She had to have a whole uncomfortable conversation to school him on dialing it down a notch. He did...but in exchange, he asked her to try a raunchy thing or two as a compromise. It took about ten rounds of this before they finally got the proportions right. Oh, and they did a weekend couples workshop on intimate communication for good measure. Kudos to them for toughing it out for that long.

Balance is the key.

The tendency of opposites is to go to extremes. But to make this relationship work, you'll need to balance out your glaring differences. An Aries we know has an on-and-off friendship with a Libra as a result of this combination's polarizing effect. When it's balanced, the go-getter Aries kicks the procrastinating Libra into gear, while the soothing Libra calms the Aries' anxiety. They're the ultimate tag team. But on a bad day, it's a showdown between aggressive, diva-style Aries tantrums and prim, white-gloved Libra haughtiness. Ugly!

Time after time, they have to go back into their corners and cool down for a couple days (sometimes weeks). Then, there's a long conversation to hash out common ground and make compromises. The Aries promises not to yell if the Libra agrees to stop showing up two hours late for everything. They eventually mess up and have to reestablish these guidelines all over again. With opposite combos, it's always a work in progress.

Get comfortable under the microscope.

Since your opposite sign has the advantage of a long-distance

"THE TENDENCY OF OPPOSITES IS TO GO TO EXTREMES. BUT TO MAKE THIS RELATIONSHIP WORK, YOU'LL NEED TO BALANCE OUT YOUR GLARING DIFFERENCES."

view of you, they can see things about you that you can't. While this can be amazingly helpful when you're receptive to it, it's also like living with a life coach 24/7, forever under the microscope. Some days, you just want them to get out of your hair and stop analyzing you, even if it's well-intended. Analyze this, buddy!

In opposite-sign combos, you may hear some advice or observations that hit you like a splash of ice-cold water. Mostly, it's because they're true—but ouch. Here you thought you were doing such a good job hiding those skeletons from the world. Who snuck in and gave this person a key to your diary?

To deal, you must give up self-consciousness (no easy feat) and accept that you're human, fallible, and have room for improvement. Be "coachable." But also, be polite. Ask if the other one is open to feedback before you point out that her non-returnable $3,000 red couture gown is actually not that flattering. Check the emotional temperature before you deliver a scathing critique of your business partner's Powerpoint presentation.

Take over the universe together.

One word: Brangelina. Although their fated connection ended, for 12 glorious years, they gave us life with their opposite-sign portmanteau perfection. Where would this Sagittarius (him)-Gemini (her) couple have been without Maddox, Zahara, Pax, Shiloh, Knox and Vivienne? Without refugee camps and orphanages and flood-ravaged cities to rebuild? Probably on separate movie lots, fondly recalling the good times they had filming Mr. and Mrs. Smith—if they remembered each other at all. ✳

LESSONS OF THIS RELATIONSHIP

• To see yourself from an enlightening "birds-eye-view" distance

• To create a powerful tag team

• To join forces and create something bigger than the two of you

• To balance extremes in yourself, like selflessness or selfishness, too much independence or dependence

• To discover a new, inspiring perspective on life

• To develop the art of compromise

Compatability

CHEAT

SHEET

Distance	Energy	The Lesson
Same Sign (**Conjunct**)	Self-acceptance	•To see your qualities mirrored back •Ease •Self-acceptance •Working through sibling rivalry
1 Sign Apart (**Inconjunct**)	Friction	•Deep healing and transformation •To learn from each other's differences •To force you out of your comfort zone •Growth through challenge or contrast
2 Signs Apart (**Sextile**)	Friendship	•To be "best friends with benefits" •How to speak up, listen, and be heard •Romance forming naturally out of friendship • Easy communication in a relationship
3 Signs Apart (**Square**)	Tension, power struggles	•Compromise •Conflict resolution •Where you can be stubborn and unyielding •Healing old wounds/parent issues
4 Signs Apart (**Trine**)	Harmony, ease	•To feel at home with yourself and a mate •To be understood without explaining yourself •To relax and play together •To have a best friend and partner in one
5 Signs Apart (**Quincunx**)	Adjustment, karma	•Karmic repair • Healing a "past life contract" •Diving into deeper intimacy •Learning to serve/give •How to adjust to someone vastly different
6 Signs Apart (**Opposite**)	Compromise, balance	•To see yourself as others do •To create something bigger than you both •To balance extremes in yourself •To discover a new perspective on life

Meet

YOUR

MATCHES

1 SIGN APART (Semisextile) – Friction

Aries: Pisces, Taurus
Taurus: Aries, Gemini
Gemini: Taurus, Cancer
Cancer: Gemini, Leo

Leo: Cancer, Virgo
Virgo: Leo, Libra
Libra: Virgo, Scorpio
Scorpio: Libra, Sag

Sag: Scorpio, Capricorn
Aquarius: Capricorn, Pisces
Capricorn: Sag, Aquarius
Pisces: Aquarius, Aries

2 SIGNS APART (Sextile) – Ease

Aries: Gemini, Aquarius
Taurus: Cancer, Pisces
Gemini: Aries, Leo
Cancer: Taurus, Virgo

Leo: Gemini, Libra
Virgo: Cancer, Scorpio
Libra: Leo, Sagittarius
Scorpio: Virgo, Capricorn

Sagittarius: Libra, Aquarius
Capricorn: Scorpio, Pisces
Aquarius: Sagittarius, Aries
Pisces: Capricorn, Taurus

3 SIGNS APART (Square) – Challenge

Aries: Cancer, Capricorn
Taurus: Aquarius, Leo
Gemini: Pisces, Virgo
Cancer: Aries, Libra

Leo: Taurus, Scorpio
Virgo: Gemini, Sagittarius
Libra: Cancer, Capricorn
Scorpio: Leo, Aquarius

Sagittarius: Virgo, Pisces
Capricorn: Aries, Libra
Aquarius: Scorpio, Taurus
Pisces: Gemini, Sagittarius

4 SIGNS APART (Trine) – Harmony

Fire: Aries-Leo-Sagittarius
Earth: Taurus-Virgo-Capricorn

Air: Gemini-Libra-Aquarius
Water: Cancer-Scorpio-Pisces

5 SIGNS APART (Quincunx) – Adjustment

Aries: Virgo, Scorpio
Taurus: Libra, Sagittarius
Gemini: Scorpio, Capricorn

Cancer: Sag, Aquarius
Leo: Capricorn, Pisces
Virgo: Aquarius, Aries

Libra: Pisces, Taurus
Scorpio: Aries, Gemini
Sagittarius: Taurus, Cancer

6 SIGNS APART (Opposite) – Perspective

Aries-Libra
Taurus-Scorpio

Gemini-Sagittarius
Cancer-Capricorn

Leo-Aquarius
Virgo-Pisces

Ophira & Tali Edut

Dubbed the "astrologers to the stars," identical twin sisters Ophira and Tali Edut, known as the AstroTwins, are professional astrologers who reach millions worldwide through their spot-on predictions. Through their website, Astrostyle. com, Ophira and Tali help "bring the stars down to earth" with their unique, lifestyle-based approach to astrology. They are also the official astrologers for ELLE Magazine and MindBodyGreen.

The AstroTwins have been featured in the UK Sunday Times, the New York Times Sunday Styles section, People Magazine and have collaborated with major brands including Vogue, Nordstrom, Revlon, H&M, Urban Outfitters, Ted Baker, Kate Spade and

Coach. The sisters have worked with celebrities including Beyoncé, Stevie Wonder, Emma Roberts, and Karlie Kloss.

They are regular guests on SiriusXM and have appeared on Bravo's The Real Housewives of New Jersey, doing on-air readings for the cast. They have authored four print books: Astrostyle, Love Zodiac, Shoestrology and Momstrology (their #1 Amazon best-selling astrological parenting guide) and a growing collection of ebooks, including their annual Planetary Planner horoscope guides. ✳

• •

VISIT THE ASTROTWINS AT
WWW.ASTROSTYLE.COM
@ASTROTWINS

Please share this book.

Like what you read? We invite you to share it with anyone and everyone you think it will help. We're passionate about ending unnecessary human conflict, and helping people have great relationships. So pass this along liberally!

Made in the USA
Columbia, SC
30 June 2018